KELVIN SMITH

How to Invest in the Stock Market for Beginners

This book was professionally typeset on Reedsy.
Find out more at reedsy.com

Contents

Introduction

Embarking on the journey of investing in the stock market is akin to setting sail on a voyage of financial discovery, where the winds of opportunity whisper promises of prosperity and the currents of knowledge chart a course towards wealth accumulation. For beginners, navigating the vast expanse of the stock market can seem daunting, with its labyrinthine complexities and fluctuating tides of uncertainty. Yet, beneath the surface lies a realm of boundless potential, where prudent decisions and strategic insights can unlock the gates to financial independence and security.

In this guide, we invite you to embark on a voyage of enlightenment and empowerment—a journey that will demystify the enigmatic world of stock market investing and equip you with the tools, knowledge, and confidence to navigate its waters with skill and resilience. Whether you are a novice investor taking your first tentative steps into the realm of equities or a seasoned trader seeking to refine your craft, this guide will serve as your compass, guiding you towards the shores of investment success.

From understanding the fundamentals of investing to mastering the art of portfolio diversification, each chapter of this guide will illuminate a different facet of the stock market landscape, offering insights, strategies, and practical advice to empower you on your journey. Whether you aspire to build a nest egg for retirement, fund your children's education, or simply grow your wealth for the future, the principles and techniques outlined in this guide will serve as your roadmap to financial prosperity.

But remember, like any voyage of discovery, investing in the stock market requires patience, perseverance, and a willingness to embrace both the triumphs and tribulations that lie ahead. There will be storms to weather, waves to ride, and unforeseen challenges to overcome. Yet, it is in these moments of adversity that the seeds of growth are sown, and the foundations of financial resilience are forged.

So, as we embark on this odyssey together, let us cast aside fear and hesitation, and embrace the boundless possibilities that await us in the world of stock market investing. With courage as our compass and knowledge as our guiding star, let us set sail towards a future of financial freedom, where the shores of prosperity beckon and the horizon of opportunity stretches endlessly before us.

1

Understanding the Basics

Investing in the stock market can seem like a daunting endeavor for beginners, but with a solid understanding of the basics, it becomes more approachable and potentially rewarding. In this chapter, we'll delve into the fundamental concepts that form the cornerstone of successful stock market investing.

1.1 Introduction to Investing

Investing is the process of allocating resources, typically money, with the expectation of generating returns over time. It involves putting money into various financial instruments, such as stocks, bonds, mutual funds, and real estate, with the goal of increasing wealth or achieving specific financial objectives. Investing differs from saving, which involves setting aside money in low-risk, interest-bearing accounts with the primary aim of preserving capital.

At its core, investing is about taking calculated risks in pursuit of potential rewards. By putting money to work in the financial markets, investors aim to grow their wealth through capital appreciation, dividends, or interest income. However, it's essential to recognize that investing carries inherent risks, and success is not guaranteed.

1.2 Why Invest in the Stock Market?

The stock market, also known as the equity market, is one of the most popular avenues for long-term wealth creation. Unlike other investment options, such as bonds or savings accounts, stocks offer the potential for significant returns over time. Historically, the stock market has delivered average annual returns that outpace inflation, making it an attractive option for investors seeking growth.

One of the primary reasons to invest in the stock market is its potential for high returns. While individual stock prices can be volatile in the short term, over the long term, stocks have historically provided substantial returns compared to other asset classes. Additionally, investing in stocks allows investors to participate in the ownership and growth of publicly traded companies, providing opportunities for wealth accumulation through capital appreciation and dividends.

1.3 Risks and Rewards of Stock Market Investing

While the stock market offers the potential for high returns, it also comes with inherent risks. Stock prices can be volatile, fluctuating in response to various factors such as economic conditions, company performance, geopolitical events, and investor sentiment. As a result, investors may experience periods of significant price swings, including both gains and losses.

One of the key risks of stock market investing is the possibility of capital loss. Unlike savings accounts or bonds, which offer principal protection, investing in stocks exposes investors to the risk of losing a portion or all of their invested capital. Market downturns, economic recessions, or company-specific issues can lead to declines in stock prices, causing financial losses for investors.

However, alongside these risks come potential rewards. Over the long term, stocks have historically delivered higher returns compared to other asset classes, such as bonds or cash equivalents. Additionally, investing in a diversified portfolio of stocks can help mitigate individual company or sector-specific risks, spreading risk across different investments and potentially improving overall investment returns.

1.4 Setting Realistic Expectations

Setting realistic expectations is essential for successful stock market investing. While the allure of high returns may be enticing, it's crucial to understand that investing is not a get-rich-quick scheme. Instead, it's a long-term endeavor that requires patience, discipline, and a well-thought-out investment strategy.

Investors should recognize that stock market returns can vary significantly from year to year and that short-term fluctuations are a normal part of investing. Setting realistic return expectations based on historical market performance and considering individual risk tolerance and investment objectives can help investors avoid disappointment and stick to their long-term investment plans.

Moreover, investors should be prepared for the possibility of market downturns and be willing to stay invested through periods of volatility. Attempting to time the market or reacting emotionally to short-term price movements can often lead to poor investment decisions. Instead, focusing on long-term goals, maintaining a diversified portfolio, and periodically re-balancing investments can help investors stay on track towards achieving financial success.

In essence, understanding the basics of investing lays the

groundwork for a successful journey in the stock market. By grasping fundamental concepts, recognizing the risks and rewards, and setting realistic expectations, beginners can embark on their investment journey with confidence and clarity.

2

Getting Started

Embarking on the journey of investing in the stock market requires careful planning and preparation. In this chapter, we will explore the essential steps involved in getting started with investing, from assessing your financial situation to choosing the right brokerage account.

2.1 Assessing Your Financial Situation

Before diving into the world of investing, it's crucial to assess your current financial situation thoroughly. This involves taking stock of your income, expenses, assets, and liabilities to gain a clear understanding of your financial health. Start by creating a comprehensive list of your sources of income, including salaries, bonuses, and any other forms of earnings. Next, calculate your monthly expenses, including rent or mortgage payments, utilities, groceries, transportation, and discretionary spending.

Once you have a clear picture of your income and expenses, assess your assets and liabilities. Assets may include savings accounts, retirement accounts, real estate, and other investments, while liabilities encompass debts such as mortgages, car loans, student loans, and credit card balances. Calculate your net worth by subtracting your total liabilities from your total assets.

Assessing your financial situation allows you to determine how much money you can allocate towards investing without jeopardizing your financial stability. It also helps identify areas where you can potentially cut expenses or increase income to free up additional funds for investing.

2.2 Establishing Investment Goals

With a clear understanding of your financial situation, the next step is to establish your investment goals. What do you hope to achieve by investing in the stock market? Are you saving for retirement, a down payment on a house, or your children's education? Setting specific, measurable, achievable, relevant, and time-bound (SMART) investment goals provides clarity and motivation for your investment journey.

Begin by identifying your short-term, medium-term, and long-term financial objectives. Short-term goals may include building an emergency fund or saving for a vacation, while medium-term goals could involve purchasing a car or funding home renovations. Long-term goals typically revolve around retirement planning and wealth accumulation.

Once you've established your investment goals, quantify the amount of money you'll need to achieve each objective and the time horizon for achieving it. This information will guide your investment strategy and asset allocation decisions, helping you tailor your portfolio to meet your specific needs and risk tolerance.

2.3 Creating a Budget for Investing

Creating a budget for investing is essential for allocating your financial resources effectively and ensuring that you stay on track towards achieving your investment goals. Start by determining how much money you can comfortably invest each month after covering essential expenses, debt payments, and savings contributions.

Consider adopting a percentage-based approach to budgeting, allocating a specific percentage of your income towards different financial priorities. For example, you might allocate 50% of your income to essentials such as housing, food, and transportation, 20% to savings and debt repayment, and 30% to discretionary spending and investing.

Automating your investment contributions can help make investing a consistent habit and remove the temptation to spend money earmarked for investing. Set up automatic transfers from your checking account to your investment accounts on a regular basis, such as monthly or bi-weekly, to ensure that you consistently contribute to your investment portfolio.

Regularly review and adjust your investment budget as your financial situation evolves and your investment goals change. Consider increasing your investment contributions as your income grows or reallocating funds from discretionary spending categories to prioritize long-term savings and investing.

2.4 Choosing the Right Brokerage Account

Choosing the right brokerage account is a critical decision that can impact your investment experience and outcomes. A brokerage account serves as a gateway to the stock market, allowing you to buy and sell stocks, bonds, mutual funds, exchange-traded funds (ETFs), and other securities.

When selecting a brokerage account, consider factors such as fees and commissions, investment options, research and educational resources, trading platforms, customer service, and account features. Compare brokerage firms to find one that aligns with your investment goals, preferences, and level of expertise.

Fee structures vary among brokerage firms, with some charging commission fees on trades and others offering commission-free trading. Evaluate the cost of trading, including commissions, account maintenance fees, and other charges, to minimize expenses and maximize investment returns.

In addition to fees, consider the investment options available through the brokerage account. Choose a brokerage that offers a diverse selection of investment products, including stocks, bonds, ETFs, and mutual funds, to build a well-rounded investment portfolio that aligns with your risk tolerance and investment objectives.

Research and educational resources provided by the brokerage can also enhance your investment knowledge and decision-making capabilities. Look for brokerages that offer comprehensive market analysis, investment research reports, educational articles, webinars, and other tools to help you make informed investment decisions.

Evaluate the trading platform and mobile app offered by the brokerage to ensure it is user-friendly, intuitive, and equipped with essential features such as real-time market data, customizable watchlists, advanced charting tools, and order execution capabilities.

Customer service and account features are also important considerations when choosing a brokerage account. Opt for a brokerage that provides responsive customer support via phone, email, or live chat, as well as access to account management features such as automatic dividend reinvestment, tax-efficient investing options, and retirement account options.

In conclusion, getting started with investing requires careful consideration of your financial situation, investment goals, budgeting strategies, and choice of brokerage account. By assessing your finances, setting SMART investment goals, creating a budget for investing, and choosing the right brokerage account, you can lay the foundation for a successful investment journey.

3

Building a Foundation

Building a solid foundation is crucial for success in the stock market. In this chapter, we will explore the essential elements of building a strong investment foundation, including an introduction to stocks, understanding market indices, and exploring different investment strategies such as value and growth investing.

3.1 Introduction to Stocks

Stocks, also known as equities, represent ownership shares in a publicly traded company. When you buy shares of stock, you become a partial owner of the company and are entitled to a portion of its profits and assets. Stocks are bought and sold on stock exchanges, such as the New York Stock Exchange (NYSE) or the NASDAQ, where investors can trade shares of publicly listed companies.

Stocks offer investors the potential for capital appreciation and income in the form of dividends. As companies grow and become more profitable, the value of their stock typically increases, allowing investors to realize gains when they sell their shares. Additionally, many companies distribute a portion of their earnings to shareholders in the form of dividends, providing investors with a regular income stream.

There are two main types of stocks: common stock and preferred stock. Common stock represents the majority of shares issued by a company and typically carries voting rights, allowing shareholders to participate in corporate governance decisions such as electing the board of directors. Preferred stock, on the other hand, typically does not carry voting rights but offers priority over common stockholders in the payment of dividends and liquidation proceeds.

Investing in stocks requires careful research and analysis to identify companies with strong fundamentals, growth potential, and attractive valuations. Investors should consider factors such as the company's financial health, competitive position, industry trends, management team, and growth prospects when evaluating potential investment opportunities.

3.2 Types of Stocks: Common vs. Preferred

Common and preferred stocks are the two primary types of stocks available to investors, each with its own characteristics and benefits.

Common stock represents ownership in a corporation and typically carries voting rights, allowing shareholders to participate in corporate governance decisions such as electing the board of directors and approving major corporate actions. Common stockholders also have the potential to receive dividends, although dividends are not guaranteed and may vary depending on the company's financial performance and dividend policy.

Preferred stock, on the other hand, represents a hybrid security that combines features of both stocks and bonds. Preferred stockholders receive priority over common stockholders in the payment of dividends and liquidation proceeds, making preferred stock more similar to bonds in terms of income generation and capital preservation. However, preferred stockholders generally do not have voting rights and may have limited upside potential compared to common stockholders.

When deciding between common and preferred stocks, investors should consider their investment objectives, risk tolerance, and income needs. Common stocks are generally more suitable for investors seeking long-term capital appreciation and growth, while preferred stocks may be more suitable for investors seeking stable income and lower volatility.

3.3 Understanding Market Indices

Market indices play a crucial role in the stock market by providing benchmarks for measuring the performance of various segments of the market. A market index is a hypothetical portfolio of securities that represents a particular market or sector, allowing investors to track the overall performance of the market or specific segments of the market over time.

The most widely followed market index in the United States is the S&P 500, which tracks the performance of 500 large-cap U.S. companies across multiple sectors. The S&P 500 is considered a barometer of the U.S. stock market and is often used as a benchmark for comparing the performance of individual stocks and investment portfolios.

Other popular market indices include the Dow Jones Industrial Average (DJIA), which tracks the performance of 30 large-cap U.S. companies, and the NASDAQ Composite, which tracks the performance of more than 2,500 U.S. and international companies listed on the NASDAQ stock exchange.

Market indices serve several purposes for investors, including measuring market performance, tracking investment returns, and evaluating investment strategies. Investors can use market indices to gauge the relative strength or weakness of different sectors of the market, identify trends and patterns, and make informed investment decisions based on market data and analysis.

3.4 Investment Strategies: Value vs. Growth Investing

Investment strategies play a crucial role in determining investment outcomes and shaping portfolio performance. Two popular investment strategies employed by investors are value investing and growth investing, each with its own approach to selecting stocks and generating investment returns.

Value investing is a strategy that focuses on identifying undervalued stocks trading at prices below their intrinsic value. Value investors seek to purchase stocks of companies that are trading at a discount to their intrinsic value, as determined by fundamental analysis of factors such as earnings, book value, cash flow, and dividends. By purchasing stocks at a discount, value investors aim to realize capital appreciation as the market recognizes and corrects the undervaluation over time.

Growth investing, on the other hand, is a strategy that focuses on identifying stocks of companies with strong growth potential and prospects for above-average earnings growth. Growth investors seek to invest in companies that are expected to grow their revenues, earnings, and market share at a faster rate than the overall market or industry. These companies typically reinvest their earnings into expanding operations, developing new products and services, and capturing market opportunities, driving long-term capital appreciation for investors.

Both value and growth investing have their strengths and weaknesses, and investors may choose to incorporate elements of both strategies into their investment approach. Value investing offers the potential for buying stocks at discounted prices and realizing capital appreciation as the market corrects the undervaluation, while growth investing offers the potential for investing in companies with strong growth prospects and realizing capital appreciation as the companies grow and expand their operations.

In summary, building a solid foundation in the stock market involves understanding the basics of stocks, exploring different types of stocks such as common and preferred, familiarizing yourself with market indices, and exploring different invest-ment strategies such as value and growth investing. By building a strong foundation, investors can lay the groundwork for successful investing and achieve their financial goals over time.

4

Fundamental Analysis

Fundamental analysis is a critical tool for investors seeking to evaluate the intrinsic value of a stock and make informed investment decisions. In this chapter, we will delve into the key components of fundamental analysis, including understanding financial statements, evaluating company performance, identifying undervalued stocks, and utilizing ratios and metrics.

4.1 Understanding Financial Statements

Financial statements are the primary source of information for investors to assess a company's financial health, performance, and profitability. The three main financial statements are the income statement, balance sheet, and cash flow statement, each providing valuable insights into different aspects of a company's operations and financial condition.

The income statement, also known as the profit and loss statement, summarizes a company's revenues, expenses, and net income over a specific period, typically quarterly or annually. It provides investors with a snapshot of a company's profitability and ability to generate earnings from its core business operations.

The balance sheet provides a snapshot of a company's financial position at a specific point in time, detailing its assets, liabilities, and shareholders' equity. Assets represent the resources owned or controlled by the company, such as cash, inventory, property, plant, and equipment, while liabilities represent the company's obligations, such as loans, accounts payable, and accrued expenses. Shareholders' equity represents the residual interest in the company's assets after deducting its liabilities and reflects the owners' claim on the company's assets.

The cash flow statement tracks the flow of cash in and out of a company during a specific period, categorizing cash flows into operating, investing, and financing activities. Operating activities include cash flows from the company's core business operations, such as sales revenue, expenses, and taxes. Investing activities include cash flows from buying or selling long-term assets, such as property, plant, and equipment, or investments in securities. Financing activities include cash flows from raising capital, such as issuing or repurchasing stock, and borrowing or repaying debt.

Understanding financial statements allows investors to assess a company's financial health, profitability, liquidity, solvency, and efficiency. By analyzing key financial metrics and trends, investors can identify strengths and weaknesses, evaluate growth prospects, and make informed investment decisions based on sound financial analysis.

4.2 Evaluating Company Performance

Evaluating company performance involves analyzing a company's financial statements, key performance indicators (KPIs), and operating metrics to assess its overall financial health and operational efficiency. Investors use various tools and techniques to evaluate company performance, including trend analysis, ratio analysis, and comparative analysis.

Trend analysis involves examining historical financial data to identify patterns, trends, and changes over time. By analyzing trends in revenue, expenses, net income, and other financial metrics, investors can assess a company's growth trajectory, profitability, and financial stability.

Ratio analysis involves calculating and interpreting financial ratios to assess a company's liquidity, solvency, profitability, efficiency, and valuation. Commonly used financial ratios include liquidity ratios (e.g., current ratio, quick ratio), solvency ratios (e.g., debt-to-equity ratio, interest coverage ratio), profitability ratios (e.g., gross profit margin, net profit margin), efficiency ratios (e.g., inventory turnover, accounts receivable turnover), and valuation ratios (e.g., price-to-earnings ratio, price-to-book ratio).

Comparative analysis involves comparing a company's financial performance and operating metrics to those of its industry peers, competitors, or benchmarks. By benchmarking against industry averages or leading competitors, investors can assess a company's relative performance, identify areas of strength and weakness, and make informed investment decisions based on relative valuation and competitive positioning.

4.3 Identifying Undervalued Stocks

Identifying undervalued stocks is a key objective of fundamental analysis, as undervalued stocks have the potential to generate above-average returns when their market price eventually reflects their intrinsic value. There are several approaches to identifying undervalued stocks, including valuation analysis, qualitative assessment, and contrarian investing.

Valuation analysis involves estimating the intrinsic value of a stock based on its fundamentals, such as earnings, cash flow, dividends, and growth prospects. Common valuation methods include discounted cash flow (DCF) analysis, dividend discount models (DDM), price-to-earnings (P/E) ratio analysis, price-to-book (P/B) ratio analysis, and enterprise value-to-EBITDA (EV/EBITDA) ratio analysis. By comparing a stock's market price to its intrinsic value, investors can identify stocks that are trading below their fair value and may be considered undervalued.

Qualitative assessment involves evaluating qualitative factors such as industry dynamics, competitive positioning, manage-ment quality, brand reputation, and growth potential. Compa-nies with strong competitive advantages, innovative products or services, and capable management teams may be undervalued by the market if their potential for future growth and profitabil-ity is not fully reflected in their current stock price.

Contrarian investing involves taking a contrarian approach to investing by buying stocks that are out of favor or trading at depressed prices due to temporary setbacks, negative senti-ment, or market overreaction. Contrarian investors believe that market inefficiencies and investor psychology can create mispricings and opportunities to buy undervalued stocks at bargain prices before they rebound.

4.4 Utilizing Ratios and Metrics

Ratios and metrics are valuable tools for fundamental analysis, providing insights into a company's financial health, perfor-mance, and valuation. Investors use a variety of ratios and metrics to assess different aspects of a company's operations and make informed investment decisions.

Liquidity ratios, such as the current ratio and quick ratio, measure a company's ability to meet its short-term obligations and cover its current liabilities with its current assets. A high liquidity ratio indicates that a company has sufficient liquid assets to cover its short-term liabilities, while a low liquidity ratio may signal liquidity risk or financial distress.

Solvency ratios, such as the debt-to-equity ratio and interest coverage ratio, measure a company's ability to meet its long-term obligations and service its debt. A low debt-to-equity ratio indicates that a company has a conservative capital structure with a low level of debt relative to equity, while a high debt-to-equity ratio may indicate higher financial leverage and greater risk of default.

Profitability ratios, such as the gross profit margin and net profit margin, measure a company's ability to generate profits from its operations. A high profitability ratio indicates that a company is effectively managing its costs and generating healthy profits, while a low profitability ratio may indicate inefficiency or competitive pressures.

Efficiency ratios, such as inventory turnover and accounts receivable turnover, measure a company's ability to manage its assets and generate revenue. A high efficiency ratio indicates that a company is efficiently utilizing its assets to generate sales, while a low efficiency ratio may indicate excess inventory or slow collections.

Valuation ratios, such as the price-to-earnings ratio and price-to-book ratio, measure a company's valuation relative to its earnings, book value, or other financial metrics. A low valuation ratio may indicate that a company is undervalued relative to its fundamentals, while a high valuation ratio may indicate that a company is overvalued and may be susceptible to a price correction.

In essence, fundamental analysis is a powerful tool for investors seeking to evaluate the intrinsic value of a stock and make informed investment decisions. By understanding financial statements, evaluating company performance, identifying undervalued stocks, and utilizing ratios and metrics, investors can build a solid foundation for successful investing and achieve their financial goals over time.

5

Technical Analysis

Technical analysis is a widely used approach to analyzing financial markets and making investment decisions based on historical price data, volume, and other market-related information. In this chapter, we will explore the key components of technical analysis, including an introduction to technical analysis, chart patterns and trends, indicators and oscillators, and developing a trading plan.

5.1 Introduction to Technical Analysis

Technical analysis is a methodology used by traders and investors to analyze historical price data and identify patterns, trends, and signals that may indicate future price movements. Unlike fundamental analysis, which focuses on evaluating a company's financial health and intrinsic value, technical analysis relies primarily on price and volume data to make investment decisions.

At the heart of technical analysis is the belief that market prices reflect all available information and that price movements follow recognizable patterns and trends over time. By studying historical price charts and applying technical indicators and tools, analysts attempt to forecast future price movements and identify trading opportunities.

Technical analysis is based on several key principles, including the efficient market hypothesis, which posits that market prices reflect all available information and are therefore random and unpredictable. However, technical analysts believe that while markets may be efficient in the long run, they are often subject to short-term trends and patterns that can be exploited for profit.

Another key principle of technical analysis is the idea of trend-following, which suggests that prices tend to move in trends or directional patterns over time. By identifying and following trends, traders can capitalize on price momentum and profit from upward or downward price movements.

Technical analysis encompasses a wide range of tools, techniques, and methodologies, including chart patterns, technical indicators, oscillators, and statistical analysis. These tools are used to analyze price data, identify trends and reversals, and generate trading signals that inform buy or sell decisions.

5.2 Chart Patterns and Trends

Chart patterns and trends are fundamental components of technical analysis, providing valuable insights into market psychology, sentiment, and supply and demand dynamics. By studying price charts and identifying patterns and trends, analysts can anticipate future price movements and make informed trading decisions.

One of the most basic concepts in technical analysis is the idea of support and resistance levels, which represent price levels at which buying or selling pressure is expected to emerge. Support levels act as floors that prevent prices from falling further, while resistance levels act as ceilings that prevent prices from rising higher. By identifying support and resistance levels on price charts, traders can anticipate potential price reversals and identify entry and exit points for trades.

Another key concept in technical analysis is the identification of chart patterns, which are recurring formations or configurations that appear on price charts and may indicate future price movements. Common chart patterns include trendlines, channels, triangles, flags, pennants, and head and shoulders patterns. By recognizing these patterns and their associated price behavior, traders can anticipate potential price breakouts or breakdowns and adjust their trading strategies accordingly.

Trend analysis is another essential component of technical analysis, as trends represent the directional movement of prices

27

over time. Trends can be classified as uptrends, downtrends, or sideways trends, depending on the direction of price movement. By identifying trends and their characteristics, traders can align their trades with the prevailing market direction and increase the probability of success.

5.3 Indicators and Oscillators

Indicators and oscillators are technical tools used to analyze price data and generate trading signals based on mathematical calculations and formulas. These tools measure various aspects of price movement, momentum, volatility, and market breadth, providing traders with additional insights into market dynamics and potential trading opportunities.

Common technical indicators include moving averages, relative strength index (RSI), moving average convergence divergence (MACD), stochastic oscillator, and Bollinger Bands. Moving averages are trend-following indicators that smooth out price data to identify the underlying trend direction. RSI is a momentum oscillator that measures the speed and change of price movements to assess overbought or oversold conditions. MACD is a trend-following momentum indicator that signals changes in the strength and direction of a trend. Stochastic oscillator is a momentum indicator that measures the location of a current price relative to its price range over a specified period. Bollinger Bands are volatility indicators that measure the standard deviation of price movements to identify potential price reversals or breakouts.

These indicators and oscillators can be used individually or in combination to confirm trading signals, filter out noise, and improve the accuracy of trading decisions. By analyzing multiple indicators and their corresponding signals, traders can gain a more comprehensive understanding of market conditions and make more informed trading decisions.

5.4 Developing a Trading Plan

Developing a trading plan is essential for success in the financial markets, as it provides a structured framework for executing trades, managing risk, and achieving trading goals. A trading plan outlines specific rules and guidelines for entering and exiting trades, managing position sizes, setting stop-loss and take-profit levels, and managing emotions and discipline.

When developing a trading plan, traders should first define their trading objectives, risk tolerance, time horizon, and capital allocation. This involves identifying specific financial goals, such as generating income, preserving capital, or achieving capital appreciation, and determining the level of risk that is acceptable for achieving those goals.

Next, traders should establish a set of trading rules and criteria for identifying trading opportunities and executing trades. This may include criteria for selecting stocks, entry and exit signals, risk management rules, and position sizing guidelines. By defining clear and objective trading rules, traders can avoid impulsive or emotional decision-making and maintain discipline and consistency in their trading approach.

Risk management is a critical component of a trading plan, as it helps protect capital and minimize losses during adverse market conditions. Traders should establish risk management rules, such as setting stop-loss orders to limit potential losses on individual trades, diversifying their portfolio to spread risk across different assets or sectors, and maintaining proper position sizing to avoid overexposure to any single trade or asset.

Finally, traders should regularly review and evaluate their trading plan to assess its effectiveness and make any necessary adjustments or refinements. This may involve analyzing trading performance, identifying strengths and weaknesses in the trading strategy, and adapting the plan to changing market conditions or personal circumstances.

In essence, technical analysis is a valuable tool for traders and investors seeking to analyze financial markets and make informed trading decisions based on historical price data and market-related information. By understanding chart patterns and trends, utilizing technical indicators and oscillators, and developing a structured trading plan, traders can enhance their trading skills, manage risk effectively, and achieve their trading goals over time.

6

Diversification and Asset Allocation

Diversification and asset allocation are cornerstone principles of prudent investing, crucial for managing risk, optimizing returns, and achieving long-term financial objectives. In this chapter, we'll delve into the significance of diversification, explore various asset allocation strategies, discuss how to construct a balanced portfolio, and emphasize the importance of regular rebalancing and monitoring of investments.

6.1 Importance of Diversification

Diversification is the strategy of spreading investments across different asset classes, industries, geographic regions, and securities to mitigate risk and enhance portfolio stability. The fundamental principle behind diversification is simple: don't put all your eggs in one basket. By allocating investments across various assets, investors can reduce the impact of adverse events affecting any single investment, sector, or market segment.

The importance of diversification stems from its ability to minimize the impact of volatility and unexpected events on investment returns. For instance, if an investor's portfolio is heavily concentrated in a single stock or sector, adverse developments such as poor financial performance or regulatory issues could significantly impact the portfolio's value. However, by diversifying across multiple stocks, sectors, and asset classes, the impact of such events can be mitigated, as losses in one area may be offset by gains in others.

Moreover, diversification allows investors to capture a broader range of investment opportunities and potential sources of returns. Different asset classes, such as stocks, bonds, real estate, and commodities, have unique risk-return profiles and respond differently to market conditions. By diversifying across these asset classes, investors can participate in various market trends and cycles, potentially enhancing portfolio returns while reducing overall risk.

Additionally, diversification helps investors achieve a more consistent and stable investment experience over time. While individual assets or sectors may experience periods of underperformance or volatility, a diversified portfolio is less susceptible to prolonged downturns or adverse market conditions. By spreading investments across different assets with low correlation, diversification smooths out the ups and downs of individual investments, resulting in a more stable and predictable investment outcome.

6.2 Asset Allocation Strategies

Asset allocation refers to the process of dividing an investment portfolio among different asset classes, such as stocks, bonds, cash, and alternative investments, based on investment objectives, risk tolerance, time horizon, and other factors. Various asset allocation strategies exist, each designed to achieve different investment goals and manage risk effectively.

One common asset allocation strategy is strategic asset allocation, which involves establishing a target asset allocation based on long-term investment objectives and maintaining that allocation through periodic rebalancing. Strategic asset allocation aims to create a well-diversified portfolio that aligns with the investor's risk tolerance and investment horizon, with the goal of achieving consistent returns over time.

Tactical asset allocation, on the other hand, involves making short-term adjustments to the portfolio's asset allocation based on changing market conditions, economic forecasts, or valuation metrics. This approach allows investors to capitalize on short-term opportunities or mitigate potential risks by adjusting the portfolio's exposure to different asset classes dynamically.

Dynamic asset allocation combines elements of both strategic and tactical asset allocation, allowing investors to adjust their asset allocation dynamically in response to changing market conditions, economic trends, or investment opportunities. This

33

approach seeks to optimize portfolio returns while managing downside risk through active management and asset allocation decisions.

Another asset allocation strategy is factor-based investing, which involves tilting the portfolio towards specific factors or investment styles that have historically provided higher returns or reduced risk. Common factors include value, growth, momentum, quality, and low volatility. By targeting specific factors, investors can potentially enhance returns or reduce risk compared to traditional market-cap-weighted strategies.

Ultimately, the most suitable asset allocation strategy depends on the investor's investment objectives, risk tolerance, time horizon, and personal preferences. It's essential to select an asset allocation strategy that aligns with these factors and to periodically review and adjust the allocation as needed based on changing circumstances and market conditions.

6.3 Building a Balanced Portfolio

Building a balanced portfolio involves selecting a mix of assets that aligns with the investor's investment goals, risk tolerance, and time horizon while diversifying across different asset classes, sectors, and geographic regions. A balanced portfolio typically includes a mix of stocks, bonds, cash, and alternative investments to achieve a blend of growth, income, and capital preservation.

Stocks are often included in a balanced portfolio to provide growth potential and capital appreciation over the long term. Stocks offer higher potential returns than other asset classes but also come with higher volatility and risk. Therefore, investors should carefully consider their risk tolerance and time horizon when allocating assets to stocks.

Bonds are another essential component of a balanced portfolio, providing income, stability, and diversification benefits. Bonds offer fixed interest payments and return of principal at maturity, making them less volatile than stocks and suitable for investors seeking income and capital preservation.

Cash and cash equivalents, such as money market funds and short-term Treasury bills, provide liquidity and stability to a balanced portfolio. Cash holdings can serve as a buffer against market volatility and provide flexibility to take advantage of investment opportunities or meet short-term liquidity needs.

Alternative investments, such as real estate, commodities, and hedge funds, can further diversify a balanced portfolio and provide exposure to non-traditional asset classes with low correlation to stocks and bonds. Alternative investments offer the potential for diversification and risk reduction, although they may also come with higher fees, complexity, and liquidity constraints.

When constructing a balanced portfolio, investors should con-sider several factors, including investment objectives, risk tolerance, time horizon, liquidity needs, tax considerations, and market conditions. By aligning the portfolio's asset allocation with these factors, investors can create a portfolio that meets their financial goals while minimizing risk.

6.4 Rebalancing and Monitoring Investments

Rebalancing and monitoring investments are essential aspects of maintaining a balanced portfolio and ensuring that it remains aligned with investment objectives and risk tolerance over time. Rebalancing involves periodically adjusting the portfolio's asset allocation to bring it back in line with the target allocation set forth in the investment plan.

Rebalancing is necessary because asset values and market conditions change over time, causing the portfolio's asset allocation to drift away from the target allocation. For example, if stocks outperform bonds over a specific period, the portfolio's allocation to stocks may increase relative to bonds, leading to higher risk exposure than intended. Rebalancing involves selling assets that have appreciated in value and reinvesting the proceeds in assets that have underperformed to restore the portfolio's target asset allocation.

Monitoring investments involves regularly reviewing the port-folio's performance, asset allocation, and investment holdings to assess their alignment with investment objectives and make any necessary adjustments or modifications. Monitoring can help investors identify changes in market conditions, economic trends, or individual investments that may warrant adjustments to the portfolio's asset allocation or investment strategy.

When rebalancing and monitoring investments, investors should consider several factors, including changes in investment objectives, risk tolerance, market conditions, economic outlook, and tax implications. By staying informed and proactive, investors can ensure that their portfolio remains on track to achieve their financial goals while minimizing risk and maximizing returns over time.

In summary, diversification and asset allocation are fundamental principles of investing that play a crucial role in managing risk, optimizing returns, and achieving long-term financial objectives. By diversifying across different asset classes, sectors, and geographic regions and allocating assets strategically based on investment objectives and risk tolerance, investors can build a balanced portfolio that is well-positioned to weather market volatility and achieve sustainable long-term growth. Regular rebalancing and monitoring of investments are essential to ensuring that the portfolio remains aligned with investment objectives and risk tolerance over time and making any necessary adjustments to optimize performance and minimize risk.

7

Investment Strategies

Investment strategies are the blueprints that guide investors in achieving their financial goals, whether they aim for long-term wealth accumulation, steady income streams, or short-term gains. In this chapter, we'll explore various investment strategies, including the distinction between long-term investing and short-term trading, the benefits of dollar-cost averaging, the principles of dividend investing, and the strategies behind growth stock investing.

7.1 Long-Term Investing vs. Short-Term Trading

Long-term investing and short-term trading represent two distinct approaches to investing, each with its own set of objectives, strategies, and risk profiles.

Long-term investing focuses on accumulating wealth over an

extended period, typically years or decades, by purchasing assets with the expectation of their value appreciating over time. Long-term investors prioritize fundamental analysis, focusing on factors such as a company's financial health, growth potential, and competitive advantages. They tend to hold investments through market fluctuations and economic cycles, aiming to benefit from the power of compounding and the long-term growth potential of the underlying assets.

Short-term trading, on the other hand, involves buying and selling assets over shorter timeframes, ranging from minutes to days or weeks, with the goal of profiting from short-term price movements. Short-term traders employ technical analysis and market timing strategies to capitalize on short-term trends, momentum, and volatility. They often use leverage and derivatives to amplify returns, but this also increases the risk of significant losses.

While both long-term investing and short-term trading can be profitable, they cater to different investment objectives and risk tolerances. Long-term investing emphasizes patience, discipline, and a focus on the underlying fundamentals of investments, while short-term trading requires quick decision-making, active monitoring of market trends, and the ability to tolerate higher levels of risk and volatility.

7.2 Dollar-Cost Averaging

Dollar-cost averaging (DCA) is an investment strategy that involves investing a fixed amount of money at regular intervals, regardless of market conditions. With DCA, investors purchase more shares when prices are low and fewer shares when prices are high, resulting in an average cost per share over time.

One of the primary benefits of dollar-cost averaging is its ability to mitigate the impact of market volatility on investment returns. By investing a fixed amount of money at regular intervals, investors automatically buy more shares when prices are low, reducing the average cost per share and potentially increasing returns when prices rebound.

Moreover, dollar-cost averaging helps investors avoid the pitfalls of trying to time the market, which can be challenging and often result in missed opportunities or losses. Instead of trying to predict market highs and lows, investors focus on consistency and discipline, steadily accumulating shares over time regardless of short-term market fluctuations.

Dollar-cost averaging is particularly well-suited for long-term investors looking to build wealth gradually over time. By investing regularly in a diversified portfolio of stocks or mutual funds, investors can benefit from the power of compounding and the long-term growth potential of the underlying assets.

However, it's important to note that dollar-cost averaging does not guarantee a profit or protect against losses in a declining market. While it can help smooth out market volatility and reduce the risk of making large investments at inopportune times, investors should still conduct thorough research and consider their investment objectives and risk tolerance before implementing this strategy.

7.3 Dividend Investing

Dividend investing is a strategy focused on investing in stocks that pay regular dividends to shareholders. Dividends are cash payments made by companies to their shareholders as a distribution of profits, typically on a quarterly or annual basis. Dividend investing appeals to investors seeking steady income streams, capital preservation, and long-term wealth accumulation.

One of the primary benefits of dividend investing is its ability to provide a reliable source of income, especially in periods of market volatility or economic uncertainty. Dividend-paying stocks tend to be more stable and defensive, as companies that consistently pay dividends often have strong cash flows, stable earnings, and a commitment to returning capital to shareholders.

Moreover, dividend investing offers the potential for both income and capital appreciation. Companies that pay dividends tend to be financially healthy and well-established, with a track record of profitability and growth. By reinvesting dividends or selecting dividend-paying stocks with the potential for long-term growth, investors can benefit from the compounding effect of reinvested dividends and the potential for capital appreciation over time.

Dividend investing also provides a degree of downside protection in bear markets, as dividends can cushion the impact of declining stock prices and provide a positive return even when capital gains are negative. Additionally, dividends are often taxed at a lower rate than interest income or capital gains, providing tax advantages for investors seeking income.

However, it's essential for dividend investors to conduct thorough research and select dividend-paying stocks based on their financial health, dividend history, payout ratio, and growth prospects. Not all dividend-paying stocks are created equal, and investors should consider factors such as industry dynamics, competitive positioning, and dividend sustainability before making investment decisions.

7.4 Growth Stock Investing

Growth stock investing is a strategy focused on investing in companies with high growth potential, often characterized by rapid revenue and earnings growth, innovative products or services, and expanding market opportunities. Growth stocks typically reinvest their earnings back into the business to fuel future growth rather than paying dividends to shareholders.

One of the primary attractions of growth stock investing is the potential for significant capital appreciation over time. Companies with strong growth prospects often outperform the broader market, generating above-average returns for investors who capitalize on their growth trajectory. By investing in growth stocks, investors can participate in the success of innovative companies and benefit from the compounding effect of long-term growth.

Moreover, growth stocks tend to be more resilient in economic downturns, as they often operate in industries with high barriers to entry, competitive advantages, and disruptive business models. Companies that continually innovate and adapt to changing market conditions are better positioned to weather economic headwinds and emerge stronger over the long term.

However, growth stock investing comes with its own set of risks and challenges. Growth stocks are often subject to higher volatility and valuation fluctuations, as their share prices may reflect high expectations for future growth. Additionally, growth companies may prioritize growth over profitability, leading to periods of negative earnings or cash flow, which can impact stock prices.

When investing in growth stocks, it's essential for investors to conduct thorough research and consider factors such as revenue growth, earnings growth, market potential, competitive positioning, and management quality. Additionally, investors should diversify their portfolio to spread risk across different sectors and industries and maintain a long-term perspective to weather short-term volatility and capitalize on the compounding effect of growth over time.

In essence, investment strategies play a crucial role in guiding investors towards their financial goals, whether they aim for long-term wealth accumulation, steady income streams, or short-term gains. Long-term investing focuses on accumulating wealth gradually over time, while short-term trading aims to profit from short-term price movements. Dollar-cost averaging helps investors mitigate market volatility and avoid trying to time the market, while dividend investing provides a reliable source of income and downside protection. Growth stock investing offers the potential for significant capital appreciation but comes with higher volatility and valuation risks. By understanding the principles behind these investment strategies and aligning them with their investment objectives and risk tolerance, investors can build a diversified portfolio that meets their financial goals and withstands market fluctuations over time.

8

Managing Risks

Risk management is a fundamental aspect of investing that involves identifying, assessing, and mitigating potential risks to protect capital and maximize returns. In this chapter, we will explore various risk management strategies, delve into the concept of volatility and its implications for investors, discuss hedging techniques to mitigate risk exposure, and emphasize the importance of patience and discipline in navigating market uncertainties.

8.1 Risk Management Strategies

Risk management strategies are designed to help investors identify, assess, and mitigate potential risks associated with their investment portfolios. While it's impossible to eliminate all investment risks entirely, effective risk management can help investors minimize losses and protect capital during adverse market conditions.

One common risk management strategy is diversification, which involves spreading investments across different asset classes, sectors, and geographic regions to reduce exposure to any single investment or risk factor. By diversifying their portfolios, investors can mitigate the impact of adverse events or fluctuations in one part of the portfolio while capturing potential gains in other parts of the portfolio.

Another risk management strategy is asset allocation, which involves determining how to distribute investment capital across different asset classes, such as stocks, bonds, cash, and alternative investments, based on investment objectives, risk tolerance, and time horizon. By diversifying their portfolios across different asset classes with low correlation, investors can reduce overall portfolio risk while potentially enhancing returns.

Additionally, investors can use risk management techniques such as stop-loss orders, which automatically sell a security when it reaches a predetermined price level, to limit potential losses on individual trades. By setting stop-loss orders, investors can protect their capital and minimize the impact of adverse price movements on their investment portfolios.

Moreover, investors can employ risk management tools such as options and futures contracts to hedge against specific risks, such as market volatility or adverse price movements. By using derivatives to offset potential losses on their investments, investors can reduce their overall risk exposure and protect their portfolios from unexpected events or market downturns.

Overall, effective risk management requires a combination of diversification, asset allocation, risk monitoring, and the use of risk management tools and techniques. By implementing a comprehensive risk management strategy, investors can protect their capital, minimize losses, and achieve their long-term investment objectives while navigating the uncertainties of the financial markets.

8.2 Understanding Volatility

Volatility refers to the degree of variation in the price of a financial asset over time and is a key measure of risk in the financial markets. High volatility indicates that the price of an asset can fluctuate significantly in a short period, while low volatility suggests that the price is relatively stable and less prone to sharp fluctuations.

Understanding volatility is essential for investors because it affects investment returns, risk exposure, and portfolio performance. High volatility can lead to significant price swings and increased uncertainty, making it challenging for investors to predict market movements and make informed investment decisions. On the other hand, low volatility can signal complacency or lack of market activity, potentially leading to decreased trading volumes and reduced investment opportunities.

One of the primary drivers of volatility in the financial markets is investor sentiment and market psychology. Fear, greed, and uncertainty can all contribute to increased volatility as investors react to changing economic conditions, geopolitical events, or corporate news. Moreover, market volatility tends to spike during periods of economic uncertainty, political instability, or financial crises, as investors reassess their risk exposure and adjust their investment strategies accordingly.

Another factor that influences volatility is market liquidity, which refers to the ease with which assets can be bought or sold without significantly impacting their price. Assets with low liquidity are more susceptible to price volatility, as even small trades can cause significant price movements. Conversely, assets with high liquidity tend to have lower volatility, as there is a larger pool of buyers and sellers willing to transact at any given price.

Additionally, external factors such as interest rates, inflation, and economic indicators can impact volatility in the financial markets. Changes in monetary policy or economic data releases can influence investor expectations and market sentiment, leading to fluctuations in asset prices and increased volatility.

While volatility can present challenges for investors, it also provides opportunities for profit and portfolio diversification. Volatility creates price movements that investors can exploit through active trading or by implementing risk management strategies such as options trading or volatility hedging. More-over, volatility can create buying opportunities for long-term investors seeking to capitalize on market dislocations or under-valued assets.

Overall, understanding volatility is essential for investors to manage risk effectively, identify investment opportunities, and navigate the complexities of the financial markets. By monitoring volatility trends, assessing their risk exposure, and implementing appropriate risk management strategies, investors can protect their capital and achieve their long-term investment goals in an uncertain market environment.

8.3 Hedging Techniques

Hedging is a risk management strategy that involves taking offsetting positions in related assets or derivatives to reduce or eliminate the risk of adverse price movements in a portfolio. Hedging allows investors to protect their portfolios from down-side risk while maintaining exposure to potential upside gains, providing a degree of insurance against unexpected events or market downturns.

One common hedging technique is using options contracts to hedge against potential losses on existing positions. For example, investors can purchase put options to protect their stock holdings from a decline in price. If the stock price falls below the strike price of the put option, the option will increase in value, offsetting the losses on the underlying stock position.

Another hedging technique is using futures contracts to hedge against changes in commodity prices, interest rates, or foreign exchange rates. Futures contracts allow investors to lock in prices for future delivery of assets, providing a hedge against price fluctuations and reducing exposure to market volatility.

Moreover, investors can use inverse exchange-traded funds (ETFs) or short-selling strategies to profit from declining markets or hedge against losses on existing positions. Inverse ETFs are designed to move in the opposite direction of their underlying index or asset, providing a hedge against market downturns. Short-selling involves borrowing shares of stock from a broker and selling them on the open market, with the intention of buying them back at a lower price to cover the position and profit from the price decline.

Additionally, investors can use diversification as a hedging technique by spreading their investments across different asset classes, sectors, and geographic regions. By diversifying their portfolios, investors can reduce the impact of adverse events or fluctuations in any single investment or risk factor, providing a degree of protection against unexpected market movements.

While hedging can help investors manage risk and protect their portfolios from adverse price movements, it also comes with costs and complexities that investors should consider. Hedging strategies often involve transaction costs, margin requirements, and the potential for imperfect correlation between hedged positions and the underlying assets, which can impact overall portfolio performance.

Moreover, hedging strategies are not foolproof and may not always be effective in mitigating all types of risks. Investors should carefully assess their risk exposure, investment objectives, and the costs and benefits of hedging before implementing hedging strategies in their portfolios.

Overall, hedging techniques can be valuable tools for investors seeking to manage risk, protect their portfolios, and achieve their long-term investment objectives. By understanding the principles behind hedging and implementing appropriate hedging strategies, investors can navigate market uncertainties and volatility with greater confidence and resilience.

8.4 Importance of Patience and Discipline

Patience and discipline are essential qualities for successful investing, particularly in a dynamic and unpredictable market environment. While it's tempting to react impulsively to short-term market fluctuations or news headlines, patient and disciplined investors understand the importance of sticking to their investment plan and maintaining a long-term perspective.

One of the key benefits of patience and discipline is the ability to avoid emotional decision-making and impulsive behavior that can lead to poor investment outcomes. In times of market volatility or uncertainty, it's natural for investors to experience fear, greed, or panic, which can cloud judgment and lead to irrational investment decisions. However, patient and disciplined investors remain focused on their long-term investment goals and resist the urge to make knee-jerk reactions to short-term market movements.

Moreover, patience and discipline enable investors to ride out market downturns and volatility without succumbing to panic selling or abandoning their investment strategy. Market fluctuations are a normal part of the investment process, and short-term volatility should not deter investors from staying committed to their long-term investment objectives. By maintaining a disciplined approach and avoiding emotional reactions to market noise, investors can avoid making costly mistakes and stay on course towards achieving their financial goals.

Furthermore, patience and discipline allow investors to take advantage of investment opportunities that may arise during periods of market dislocation or undervaluation. Contrarian investors who are willing to go against the crowd and buy assets when others are selling can often capitalize on market inefficiencies and generate attractive returns over the long term. However, this requires patience to wait for the right opportunity and discipline to stick to the investment thesis despite short-term market fluctuations.

Additionally, patience and discipline are essential for successful risk management and portfolio diversification. By adhering to a well-thought-out investment plan and maintaining a diversified portfolio, investors can reduce the impact of adverse market events and protect their capital from significant losses. However, this requires patience to stay the course during periods of market turbulence and discipline to rebalance the portfolio as needed to maintain the desired asset allocation.

In summary , patience and discipline are essential qualities for successful investing, particularly in a volatile and uncertain market environment. By remaining patient and disciplined, investors can avoid emotional decision-making, stay focused on their long-term investment goals, and take advantage of investment opportunities that may arise during market downturns. Moreover, patience and discipline are crucial for effective risk management and portfolio diversification, allowing investors to protect their capital and achieve their long-term investment objectives with confidence and resilience.

9

Psychological Aspects of Investing

Investing is not just about numbers and financial analysis; it also involves understanding and managing the psychological aspects that influence decision-making and behavior. In this chapter, we will explore the psychological aspects of investing, including overcoming emotional biases, developing a rational mindset, dealing with market volatility, and staying committed to your investment plan.

9.1 Overcoming Emotional Biases

One of the biggest challenges investors face is overcoming emotional biases that can cloud judgment and lead to irrational decision-making. Emotional biases, such as fear, greed, overconfidence, and loss aversion, can significantly impact investment decisions and result in suboptimal outcomes.

Fear and greed are two of the most common emotional biases that influence investor behavior. Fear can cause investors to panic sell during market downturns, leading to losses and missed opportunities for recovery. Conversely, greed can lead investors to chase high-flying stocks or speculative investments, ignoring the underlying risks and fundamentals.

Overconfidence is another prevalent emotional bias that can lead investors to overestimate their ability to predict market movements or pick winning investments. Overconfident investors may take excessive risks or ignore diversification principles, believing they have an edge over the market that others do not.

Loss aversion refers to the tendency of investors to prefer avoiding losses over achieving gains, leading to risk-averse behavior and missed opportunities for growth. Investors may hold onto losing investments for too long, hoping they will rebound, or sell winning investments too soon to lock in gains, resulting in suboptimal portfolio performance.

To overcome emotional biases, investors must recognize and acknowledge their existence and take steps to mitigate their impact on decision-making. This may involve implementing rules-based investment strategies, setting predefined entry and exit points, and maintaining a long-term perspective that focuses on fundamental analysis rather than short-term market fluctuations.

Moreover, investors can benefit from seeking feedback from objective sources, such as financial advisors or mentors, who can provide unbiased perspectives and help them avoid common emotional pitfalls. By staying disciplined, rational, and focused on their long-term investment goals, investors can overcome emotional biases and make informed decisions that align with their financial objectives.

9.2 Developing a Rational Mindset

Developing a rational mindset is crucial for successful investing, as it enables investors to make decisions based on logic, reason, and evidence rather than emotions or impulses. A rational mindset involves maintaining objectivity, critical thinking, and discipline in the face of uncertainty and market volatility.

One of the key principles of rational investing is conducting thorough research and analysis before making investment decisions. This may involve evaluating company fundamentals, analyzing industry trends, assessing competitive positioning, and considering macroeconomic factors that could impact investment outcomes. By basing investment decisions on sound analysis and evidence, investors can reduce the influence of emotions and make more informed choices.

Another aspect of developing a rational mindset is having a well-defined investment plan and sticking to it through market ups and downs. A written investment plan outlines specific goals, objectives, asset allocation targets, and risk management strategies, providing a roadmap for achieving long-term financial success. By adhering to their investment plan and resisting the urge to deviate from it based on short-term market fluctuations, investors can maintain discipline and avoid making impulsive decisions.

Moreover, rational investors understand the importance of diversification and risk management in achieving their investment objectives. They spread their investments across different asset classes, sectors, and geographic regions to reduce risk and enhance portfolio stability. Rational investors also implement risk management techniques, such as stop-loss orders, position sizing, and hedging strategies, to protect their capital and minimize losses during adverse market conditions.

Lastly, developing a rational mindset involves embracing uncertainty and acknowledging that investing inherently involves risks and uncertainties. Rational investors understand that they cannot control market outcomes or predict the future with certainty, but they can control their reactions and responses to market events. By maintaining a calm and rational demeanor, investors can navigate market volatility and make decisions that are consistent with their long-term financial goals.

9.3 Dealing with Market Volatility

Market volatility is a natural part of the investing process and can create both challenges and opportunities for investors. While volatility can be unsettling and unpredictable, it also provides opportunities for profit and portfolio growth for those who can navigate it effectively.

One strategy for dealing with market volatility is maintaining a long-term perspective and focusing on the fundamentals of investments rather than short-term price movements. By investing in high-quality companies with strong fundamentals, diversified revenue streams, and competitive advantages, investors can withstand short-term market fluctuations and benefit from long-term growth potential.

Moreover, investors can use volatility to their advantage by adopting a contrarian approach and buying assets when others are selling. Contrarian investors seek opportunities in undervalued or overlooked assets that have the potential for long-term appreciation once market sentiment improves. By going against the crowd and taking a patient, long-term view, contrarian investors can capitalize on market dislocations and generate attractive returns over time.

Additionally, investors can use risk management techniques such as diversification, asset allocation, and hedging to mitigate the impact of market volatility on their investment portfolios. Diversification involves spreading investments across different asset classes, sectors, and geographic regions to reduce risk and enhance portfolio stability. Asset allocation involves determining how to distribute investment capital across different asset classes based on investment objectives, risk tolerance, and time horizon. Hedging involves taking offsetting positions in related assets or derivatives to reduce or eliminate the risk of adverse price movements in a portfolio.

Furthermore, investors can benefit from maintaining liquidity in their portfolios to take advantage of investment opportunities that may arise during periods of market volatility. By keeping cash reserves or maintaining access to lines of credit, investors can capitalize on market downturns to purchase assets at discounted prices or rebalance their portfolios to take advantage of changing market conditions.

Overall, dealing with market volatility requires a combination of patience, discipline, and risk management. By maintaining a long-term perspective, focusing on the fundamentals of investments, and implementing sound risk management strategies, investors can navigate market uncertainties with confidence and resilience.

9.4 Staying Committed to Your Investment Plan

Staying committed to your investment plan is essential for achieving long-term financial success and realizing your investment objectives. While it's natural to feel tempted to deviate from your plan in response to short-term market fluctuations or external factors, staying disciplined and focused on your long-term goals is key to overcoming challenges and achieving consistent returns over time.

One of the primary benefits of staying committed to your

investment plan is maintaining consistency and discipline in the face of uncertainty and market volatility. Market fluctuations and economic uncertainties are inevitable, but by sticking to your investment plan and remaining focused on your long-term objectives, you can avoid making impulsive decisions that could derail your progress or lead to suboptimal outcomes.

Moreover, staying committed to your investment plan helps you avoid the pitfalls of market timing and emotional decision-making, which can be detrimental to long-term investment performance. Attempting to time the market by buying and selling assets based on short-term price movements or news headlines is a risky and unreliable strategy that often results in missed opportunities or losses. By adhering to your investment plan and maintaining a long-term perspective, you can avoid the temptation to react impulsively to market noise and focus on the fundamentals of investing.

Additionally, staying committed to your investment plan enables you to benefit from the power of compounding and the long-term growth potential of your investments. Consistently contributing to your investment portfolio and reinvesting dividends or interest income allows you to harness the compounding effect, where earnings generate additional earnings over time, leading to accelerated growth and wealth accumulation.

Furthermore, staying committed to your investment plan fosters a sense of confidence and conviction in your investment decisions, allowing you to weather short-term market fluctuations and uncertainties with greater resilience. By having a clear understanding of your investment objectives, risk tolerance, and time horizon, you can stay focused on your long-term goals and avoid being swayed by short-term market volatility or external factors.

In essence, staying committed to your investment plan is essential for achieving long-term financial success and realizing your investment objectives. By maintaining consistency, discipline, and focus in the face of market uncertainties, you can avoid emotional decision-making, capitalize on long-term investment opportunities, and achieve consistent returns over time. Remember that investing is a marathon, not a sprint, and staying committed to your plan will help you navigate the ups and downs of the market with confidence and resilience.

10

Monitoring and Reviewing Your Investments

Monitoring and reviewing your investments are crucial aspects of successful investing that enable you to track portfolio performance, make informed decisions, and adapt to changing market conditions. In this chapter, we will explore the importance of monitoring and reviewing your investments, including tracking portfolio performance, adjusting your investment strategy, reinvesting dividends and profits, and seeking continuous learning and improvement.

10.1 Tracking Portfolio Performance

Tracking portfolio performance is essential for investors to assess the effectiveness of their investment strategies, evaluate the success of individual investments, and identify areas for improvement. By regularly monitoring portfolio performance, investors can gain insights into their investment decisions, track progress towards their financial goals, and make informed adjustments to their investment strategy as needed.

One key aspect of tracking portfolio performance is measuring investment returns relative to benchmarks or indices that represent the broader market or specific asset classes. Comparing portfolio performance against relevant benchmarks provides investors with a benchmark for evaluating investment performance and assessing the value added by their investment decisions. For example, if a portfolio of U.S. stocks outperforms the S&P 500 index, it indicates that the portfolio has generated alpha, or excess returns, relative to the market.

Moreover, investors can use performance metrics such as return on investment (ROI), compound annual growth rate (CAGR), and volatility to assess portfolio performance and measure progress towards their investment objectives. These metrics provide valuable insights into the risk-adjusted returns, growth rate, and stability of investment portfolios, allowing investors to evaluate performance over different time periods and market conditions.

Furthermore, tracking portfolio performance involves monitoring key performance indicators (KPIs) such as asset allocation, diversification, and risk exposure to ensure that investment portfolios remain aligned with investment objectives, risk tolerance, and time horizon. By regularly reviewing KPIs, investors can identify any deviations from their target asset allocation, rebalance their portfolios as needed, and mitigate the risk of overexposure to any single investment or risk factor.

Overall, tracking portfolio performance is essential for investors to assess the effectiveness of their investment strategies, evaluate the success of individual investments, and make informed decisions to achieve their financial goals. By regularly monitoring performance metrics, comparing portfolio returns against benchmarks, and reviewing key performance indicators, investors can stay on track towards achieving long-term investment success.

10.2 Adjusting Your Investment Strategy

Adjusting your investment strategy is a crucial aspect of successful investing that allows investors to adapt to changing market conditions, capitalize on new opportunities, and mitigate risks. While having a well-defined investment plan is important, it's equally essential for investors to be flexible and willing to adjust their strategy based on evolving market dynamics and personal circumstances.

One reason investors may need to adjust their investment strategy is changes in their financial goals, risk tolerance, or time horizon. Life events such as marriage, parenthood, career changes, or retirement can impact investors' financial objectives and risk profiles, necessitating adjustments to their investment strategies to align with their evolving needs and circumstances.

Moreover, changes in market conditions, economic outlook, or regulatory environment may warrant adjustments to investment strategies to mitigate risks and capitalize on new opportunities. For example, during periods of economic uncertainty or market volatility, investors may choose to increase portfolio diversification, reduce exposure to high-risk assets, or implement risk management techniques to protect capital and preserve wealth.

Furthermore, adjustments to investment strategies may be necessary to take advantage of changes in industry trends, technological advancements, or macroeconomic factors that can impact investment opportunities and asset valuations. By staying informed about market developments and emerging trends, investors can proactively adjust their investment strategies to capitalize on new growth sectors or emerging investment themes.

Additionally, adjustments to investment strategies may involve rebalancing investment portfolios to maintain target asset allocations and risk profiles. Rebalancing involves buying or selling assets within a portfolio to restore the desired asset allocation and ensure that the portfolio remains aligned with investment objectives and risk tolerance. Rebalancing allows investors to trim overweight positions, reallocate capital to underperforming assets, and capitalize on opportunities that arise during market fluctuations.

Overall, adjusting your investment strategy is essential for investors to adapt to changing market conditions, capitalize on new opportunities, and mitigate risks. By staying flexible, informed, and proactive, investors can make informed decisions to adjust their investment strategies and achieve their financial goals in an ever-changing market environment.

10.3 Reinvesting Dividends and Profits

Reinvesting dividends and profits is a powerful strategy for accelerating wealth accumulation, maximizing investment returns, and compounding growth over time. Rather than withdrawing dividends or profits as cash, investors can reinvest them back into their investment portfolios to purchase additional shares of stock or fund units, increasing the size and value of their investments over time.

One of the primary benefits of reinvesting dividends and profits is the power of compounding, where earnings generate additional earnings over time, leading to exponential growth in investment value. By reinvesting dividends and profits, investors can take advantage of the compounding effect to accelerate wealth accumulation and achieve their financial goals faster than through capital appreciation alone.

Moreover, reinvesting dividends and profits allows investors to harness the benefits of dollar-cost averaging, where they purchase more shares when prices are low and fewer shares when prices are high, resulting in a lower average cost per share over time. By consistently reinvesting dividends and profits, investors can benefit from the volatility of the market and capitalize on opportunities to accumulate shares at attractive prices.

Furthermore, reinvesting dividends and profits can help investors maintain portfolio diversification and asset allocation targets over time. Rather than letting cash accumulate in their investment accounts, investors can reinvest dividends and profits into existing holdings or new investment opportunities to ensure that their portfolios remain aligned with their investment objectives and risk tolerance.

Additionally, reinvesting dividends and profits can provide a source of passive income and wealth accumulation, allowing investors to build a portfolio of income-generating assets over time. Dividend reinvestment plans (DRIPs) offered by many companies and mutual funds allow investors to automatically reinvest dividends into additional shares of stock or fund units without incurring transaction costs or brokerage fees, making it easy and cost-effective to reinvest dividends and profits.

Overall, reinvesting dividends and profits is a powerful strategy for accelerating wealth accumulation, maximizing investment returns, and compounding growth over time. By taking advantage of the compounding effect, harnessing the benefits of dollar-cost averaging, and maintaining portfolio diversification, investors can achieve their financial goals faster and build a secure financial future.

10.4 Seeking Continuous Learning and Improvement

Continuous learning and improvement are essential for investors to stay informed, adapt to changing market conditions, and enhance their investment skills and knowledge over time. The financial markets are dynamic and ever-evolving, and successful investors must continuously update their understanding of market dynamics, investment strategies, and economic trends to make informed decisions and achieve long-term investment success.

One way investors can seek continuous learning and improvement is by staying informed about market developments, economic trends, and industry news through various sources of information, such as financial news websites, investment publications, and market research reports. By staying up-to-date on current events and emerging trends, investors can gain valuable insights into market dynamics and identify new investment opportunities.

Moreover, investors can benefit from attending investment seminars, workshops, and conferences to learn from industry experts, gain new perspectives, and exchange ideas with fellow investors. Investment education programs offered by financial institutions, universities, and professional organizations provide opportunities for investors to deepen their understanding of investment principles, portfolio management techniques, and risk management strategies.

Furthermore, investors can seek guidance and mentorship from experienced investors or financial advisors who can provide personalized advice, insights, and recommendations based on their expertise and experience. By leveraging the knowledge and expertise of seasoned professionals, investors can gain valuable insights into market trends, investment strategies, and risk management techniques to enhance their investment performance and achieve their financial goals.

Additionally, investors can benefit from actively reviewing and analyzing their investment decisions, portfolio performance, and investment outcomes to identify areas for improvement and refine their investment approach over time. By conducting post-mortem analyses of investment successes and failures, investors can learn from past experiences, identify patterns of behavior, and make adjustments to their investment strategy to enhance future performance.

Overall, seeking continuous learning and improvement is essential for investors to stay informed, adapt to changing market conditions, and enhance their investment skills and knowledge over time. By staying informed about market developments, attending investment education programs, seeking guidance from experienced professionals, and reviewing investment decisions, investors can continuously refine their investment approach and achieve long-term investment success in an ever-changing market environment.

11

Conclusion

In the symphony of life, investing in the stock market for beginners represents a crescendo of possibility—a harmonious interplay of ambition, intellect, and opportunity. As we draw the curtain on this enlightening journey, it is essential to reflect on the lessons learned, the wisdom gained, and the path ahead.

For beginners, the stock market may initially appear as a daunting labyrinth of numbers, charts, and jargon. Yet, armed with knowledge, guidance, and perseverance, they embark on a transformative voyage—a journey of self-discovery and financial empowerment.

Throughout this guide, we have explored the fundamental principles of investing, from understanding the dynamics of the market to crafting a well-diversified portfolio. We have delved into the intricacies of risk management, the art of analysis, and the importance of patience and discipline.

But beyond the technicalities lies a deeper truth—a truth that transcends numbers and charts and resonates at the core of our being. Investing in the stock market is not merely a pursuit of financial gain; it is an expression of faith in the future—a belief in the power of human ingenuity, innovation, and progress.

As beginners navigate the tumultuous seas of the market, they will encounter challenges, setbacks, and moments of doubt. Yet, it is in these moments of adversity that the seeds of growth are sown, and the foundations of resilience are forged.

For in the journey of investing, as in the journey of life, it is not the destination that defines us but the path we tread—the lessons we learn, the obstacles we overcome, and the people we become along the way.

So, as we bid farewell to this guide and embark on our individual voyages, let us carry with us the wisdom gained, the lessons learned, and the dreams that inspire us. Let us embrace the challenges that lie ahead with courage, determination, and an unwavering belief in our ability to succeed.

For in the vast expanse of the stock market, as in the boundless depths of the human spirit, there are no limits to what we can achieve. So, let us set sail towards a future of possibility, where the shores of prosperity beckon and the horizon of opportunity stretches endlessly before us.